Suit Up!

Empowered With Purpose

Information Spiritual Warfare Study Guide

LILLIAN LAITMAN

Copyright © 2023 Lillian Laitman

Published by Fina Press, an imprint of WoW Media Publishing

www.wowmediapublishing.com

Facebook: @wowmediapublishingFB

Instagram: @wowmediapublishinglm

All rights reserved. No part of this publication may be reproduced, distributed, or transmitted in any form or by any means, including photocopying, recording, or other electronic or mechanical methods, without the prior written permission of the publisher, except in the case of brief quotations embodied in critical reviews and certain other noncommercial uses permitted by copyright law. For permission requests, contact the publisher at the email, wowmediapublishing@outlook.com, "Attention: Publications Specialist."

LCCN: 2024905538

Unless otherwise noted, all Scripture quotations are from the Holy Bible, New International Version®, NIV®. Copyright © 1973, 1978, 1984, 2011 by Biblica, Inc.® Used by permission of Zondervan. All rights reserved worldwide. www.zondervan.com. The "NIV" and "New International Version" are trademarks registered in the United States Patent and Trademark Office by Biblica, Inc.®

Scripture quotations marked AMP are from the Amplified Bible. Copyright © 2015 by The Lockman Foundation. Used by permission. www.Lockman.org.

Scripture quotations marked ESV are from the Holy Bible, English Standard Version. Copyright © 2001 by Crossway Bibles, a division of Good News Publishers. Used by permission.

Scripture quotations marked KJV are from the King James Version of the Bible.

Scripture quotations marked NKJV are taken from the New King James Version®. Copyright © 1982 by Thomas Nelson. Used by permission. All rights reserved.

Scripture quotations marked NLT are taken from the Holy Bible, New Living Translation, copyright © 1996, 2004, 2007. Used by permission of Tyndale House Publishers, Inc., Wheaton, IL 60189. All rights reserved.

ISBN: 978-1-7345942-4-9 (Paperback)
ISBN: 9781-7345942-7-0 (E-Pub)

Cover design by Lisa McClure
Back cover photo credit: Sonia Huertas Photography
Interior design: Heidi Sutherlin

A portion of the proceeds from every copy sold is donated to missions in giving back to the local community, the nation, and the world. *Honor God, Love Life, and Make Disciples*

Library of Congress Control Number: 2024905538

1 2 3 4 5 6 7 8   LSI   29 28 27 26 25 24

Contents

Preface: The Information Warfare Plan 1

Introduction: The Armor of God Is Our Strength 3

How to Use This Study Guide 7

Chapter 1: Strength Doesn't Always Look Like Wonder Woman 11

Chapter 2: Lasso the Lies With the Truth 25

Chapter 3: Become Bulletproof 35

Chapter 4: Boots on the Ground 45

Chapter 5: Take Up Your Shield 53

Chapter 6: Queen in Training 63

Chapter 7: The "god" Killer 73

Preface
The Information Warfare Plan

Modern military tactics include a strategy called *information warfare,* which has been defined as "any action to deny, exploit, corrupt, or destroy the enemy's information and its functions; protecting ourselves against those actions; and exploiting our own military information functions." As we discover how to properly suit up for the battles we face, we must also learn how to jam the enemy's lines of communication to our hearts and minds.

This is why at the end of each chapter of the main book, *Suit Up! Empowered With Purpose*, you will find an Information Warfare Plan that includes a daily Scripture verse and a focal point based upon the chapter's weapon. When we read God's Word is a powerful weapon to combat the enemy's strategies to deceive us. Prayer is also a powerful weapon in our arsenal because when we speak God's Word aloud through prayer, it activates our faith and shuts down the enemy's communication strategy.

I recommend that you take your time digesting the information in each chapter. The Scriptures provided at the end are one week's worth of verses carefully chosen so you can meditate and digest the Word of God. Instead of rushing onto the next chapter, take time daily to read the recommended

Scripture, meditate on it, pray over it, journal about what God speaks to your heart, and then when you've read all of them, move on to the next chapter.

Prayer is critical to our victory. Prayer isn't something we limit to once a week at church, or even once day when we get up in the morning. We should pray all day, every day (1 Thess. 5:16-17). Prayer isn't just kneeling for hours at a time. There are many ways you can pray. You can be driving and praying (with your eyes open!). Or you can pray a "bullet prayer"—a quick, targeted prayer—as the Holy Spirit guides you in what or who to pray for.

In whatever manner you pray, the key is that you pray. **There is power in prayer,** whether spoken aloud or in silence.

Introduction
The Armor of God Is Our Strength

As women, we often wear many different hats. On the job, we may be supervising a team of coworkers. We deal with the daily stressors of meeting goals and dodging office politics in addition to being overburdened with heavy workloads. At home, we take care of family members—our spouse, maybe children, aging parents, or extended family who need our support. We also are responsible for grocery shopping, cooking, cleaning, paying bills, doing laundry, and the list goes on. In the community, we may be committed to our local church or involved in extracurricular activities.

It's exhausting just reading it!

For these reasons, it's important we learn to walk daily in our God-given strength. Walking around in our own strength, which hasn't been proven in the fire and whose mettle hasn't been tested, leaves us vulnerable to attack and exposes our weaknesses, as in the case of my superheroine Wonder Woman.

The Bible warns us to be wary of the enemy's fiery arrows. It also says, "For the weapons of our warfare are not carnal but mighty in God for pulling down strongholds, casting down arguments and every high thing that exalts itself against the knowledge of God, bringing every thought into captivity to the obedience of Christ" (2 Cor. 10:4–5, NKJV).

Each chapter in this book will show you how to dress for battle in this unseen armor. There would appear to be six pieces of armor, but in the revelation God shared with me for this book, there are seven, which I outline in the following table.

Weapon	Its Purpose
1. Belt of Truth	Holds everything together and points to the fact that we need to be grounded in the truth of God's Word.
2. Breastplate of Righteousness	Guards our heart, the seat of our emotions, and reminds us that pursuing His righteousness helps us avoid sin.
3. Shoes of Peace	Help us to assume a "ready stance" and fight for what we know is true; also help us be prepared to share God's Word with others.
4. Shield of Faith	Blocks the enemy's fiery darts against attacks on our mind; shows that having a solid faith in God keeps us on course even in the middle of a battle.
5. Helmet of Salvation	No head, we're dead! Indicates that without salvation, there is no life in the Spirit.
6. Sword of the Spirit—God's Word	The only offensive weapon on this list; reminds us that we must be grounded in God's Word to fight temptation and spiritual attacks.
7. Sword of the Spirit—Prayer	Once we've read the Word and digested it into our spirit, we should verbalize it in prayer so that it becomes activated through our profession of faith.

This entire book is based upon this passage from Ephesians 6:

Finally, be strong in the Lord and in his mighty power. Put on the full armor of God, so that you can take your stand against the devil's schemes. For our struggle is not against flesh and blood, but against the rulers, against the authorities, against the powers of this dark world and against the spiritual forces of evil in the heavenly realms. Therefore put on the full armor of God, so that when the day of evil comes, you may be able to stand your ground, and after you have done everything, to stand. Stand firm then, with the belt of truth buckled around your waist, with the breastplate of righteousness in place, and with your feet fitted with the readiness that comes from the gospel of peace. In addition to all this, take up the shield of faith, with which you can extinguish all the flaming arrows of the evil one. Take the helmet of salvation and the sword of the Spirit, which is the word of God. And pray in the Spirit on all occasions with all kinds of prayers and requests. With this in mind, be alert and always keep on praying for all the Lord's people.

—Ephesians 6:10–18

How to Use This Study Guide

This seven-week Bible study guide based on Ephesians 6:10-18 can help you deepen your understanding of spiritual warfare and equip you with the full armor of God to face life's challenges with faith and strength. This guide is divided into seven sections, each corresponding to the armor of God as identified in the main book, *Suit Up! Empowered With Purpose*.

This guide is structured for individual or group study and includes tailored strategies for each day, to make the most of your time with God and increase your understanding of His Word. These reflection and discussion questions can enrich individual or group Bible study sessions by encouraging deeper reflection on the Scriptures and facilitating meaningful conversations about faith and application in daily life.

Monday Setting Goals and Planning

- **Reflect on previous week:** Take time to review your progress, identify areas of improvement, and celebrate your achievements.
- **Set weekly goals:** Define clear and actionable goals for the upcoming week, including specific tasks and deadlines.

- **Create a study schedule:** Plan dedicated study times based on your goals and prioritize tasks accordingly.
- **Organize study materials:** Gather all necessary resources, notes, and online materials for efficient access throughout the week.

Tuesday Active Learning and Note-taking

- **Engage in active learning:** Focus on interactive learning methods such as summarizing, paraphrasing, and applying concepts.
- **Develop effective note-taking techniques:** Experiment with various methods like mind maps or the outline method.
- **Highlight key information:** Train yourself to identify and highlight important points while reading or listening to sermons or podcasts.
- **Review and revise notes regularly:** Consolidate your understanding by revisiting your notes periodically.

Wednesday Deep Dive into Concepts

- **Dive deeper into core concepts:** Allocate generous time to thoroughly understand key concepts and principles.
- **Research and supplement knowledge:** Go beyond the book and explore additional resources. There are so many online Bible tools and resources that are completely free. Take advantage of them to glean from the Word.
- **Seek clarification:** If you encounter any uncertainties, reach out to your pastor or spiritual leader for further clarification.

Thursday Collaborative Learning

- **Form study groups:** Collaborate with friends or people at church to discuss and exchange ideas, share perspectives, and clarify doubts.
- **Conduct group discussions:** Organize study sessions where you can collectively review and teach concepts to one another.

- **Prayer partner:** Exchange contact information within the group and assign each person a prayer partner.
- **Share resources and study materials:** Create a shared repository of helpful resources to enhance the lessons learned each week.

Friday Review and Consolidation

- **Review the week's material:** Allocate time to consolidate your learning from the week, focusing on difficult topics or areas of weakness.
- **Create summary notes:** Develop condensed summaries for each subject, capturing the main ideas, and key points.
- **Use memory aids:** Utilize memory techniques like acronyms, visualization, or storytelling to aid retention.
- **Journal:** Assess your understanding by journaling thoughts/questions/ideas that resonated with you most over the week.

Saturday Application and Practice

- **Apply knowledge to real-world scenarios:** Look at ways to apply what you've learned and incorporate them into daily situations.
- **Seek feedback:** Request feedback from your professors, mentors, or peers on your work to identify areas for improvement.
- **Reflect and refine:** Analyze your performance, identify strengths and weaknesses, and make necessary adjustments.

Sunday Relaxation and Self-Care

- **Take a break:** Allow yourself time for relaxation, leisure activities, and rejuvenation.
- **Practice self-care:** Engage in activities that promote spiritual, mental, and physical well-being, such as journaling which verse, or verses, spoke to you most over the past week; get some exercise, even if it's just a 30-minute walk or pursuing hobbies that you enjoy.

- **Prepare for the upcoming week:** Schedule your Bible study time so that nothing interferes with it. Like physical exercise, spiritual exercise needs to become a regular part of your routine.

Conclusion

By implementing the strategies outlined for each day of the week, you will be better prepared to fully absorb the Word and reflect on what are the takeaways that the Holy Spirit is showing you.

Let's dive in!

Chapter 1
Strength Doesn't Always Look Like Wonder Woman

We deal with the daily stressors of meeting goals and dodging office politics in addition to being overburdened with heavy workloads. At home, we take care of family members—our spouse, maybe children, aging parents, or extended family who need our support. We also are responsible for grocery shopping, cooking, cleaning, paying bills, doing laundry, and the list goes on. In the community, we may be committed to our local church or involved in extracurricular activities.

For these reasons it's important we learn to walk daily in our God-given strength. Walking around in our own strength, which hasn't been proven in the fire and whose mettle hasn't been tested, leaves us vulnerable to attack and exposes our weaknesses, as in the case of my superheroine Wonder Woman.

We need to learn to balance all of our relationships because each person who enters our lives is there for a reason. People don't enter our lives by accident. There's a reason our worlds have collided. There is something only you can offer that others need to experience. Through our gifts and talents, we can live life out loud for God.

Recommended Daily Reading

Day 1: Ephesians 6:10–11

Day 2: Ephesians 6:12

Day 3: Ephesians 6:13

Day 4: Ephesians 6:14

Day 5: Ephesians 6:15

Day 6: Ephesians 6:16–17

Day 7: Ephesians 6:18

Day 1: Ephesians 6:10–11

Reflection

What does it mean to be strong in the Lord?

Why is it important to be aware of the devil's schemes?

How can you put on the full armor of God in your daily life?

Day 2: Ephesians 6:12

Reflection

Write down steps that you can take to stand your ground when your faith is attacked.

Discussion

What did the apostle Paul imply when he states "...and against evil spirits in the heavenly places"? (See Ephesians 2:7, 3:10-11; Daniel 10:1-13)

Who or what is our real battle against, according to this verse?

How does understanding this spiritual battle change your perspective on daily challenges and conflicts?

How can you stay grounded in your faith amidst spiritual warfare?

Day 3: Ephesians 6:13

Reflection

List examples of situations where standing firm in your faith made a difference.

Discussion

What is the significance of "standing your ground" in the face of evil?

How does putting on the full armor of God prepare you for the challenges of life?

Day 4: Ephesians 6:14

Reflection

Think about the ways you can ensure integrity is integral part of your life.

Discussion

What does the "belt of truth" represent in the full armor of God?

How does righteousness protect you spiritually?

Day 5: Ephesians 6:15

Reflection

Reflect on how the gospel brings peace into your life.

Discussion

What does it mean to have "feet fitted with the readiness of the gospel of peace"?

How can you be a peacemaker in your relationships and community?

Day 6: Ephesians 6:16–17

Reflection

Reflect on the symbolism of the shield of faith and the helmet of salvation.

Discussion

How does faith protect you from the attacks of the evil one?

How can you use the "sword of the Spirit" (the Word of God) in your daily life?

Day 7: Ephesians 6:18

Reflection

Reflect on the importance of praying for fellow believers and the broader community.

Discussion

Why is prayer a crucial aspect of spiritual warfare?

How can you incorporate regular prayer into your daily routine?

NOTES

Chapter 2
Lasso the Lies With the Truth

I find it fitting that the first piece of spiritual armor listed in Ephesians 6 is the belt of truth, because John 14:6 says Jesus is "the way, the truth, and the life" (NKJV). In Roman times, the belt played a critical role in the effectiveness of a soldier's armor. The belt was where the soldier placed his sword. Without the belt, he could be missing his most important weapon. For believers, the belt holds the sword of the Spirit, linking the truth and God's Word (John 17:17). Without understanding what truth is, we can be easily deceived (Eph. 4:14). And deception is the enemy's overarching counter-weapon to the belt of truth.

God desires truth—sincerity—in the most inward parts of our lives (Ps. 51:6). When we act with sincere hearts, walking in truth and integrity, we can stand strong.

The source of truth is Jesus Christ because He *is* the truth. Jesus said, "I am the way and *the truth* and the life. No one comes to the Father except through me" (John 14:6, emphasis added). And in coming to know Jesus on a personal level, you begin to understand He is the truth who sets you free from the shackles of sin and the burdens this world piles on your shoulders.

Recommended Daily Reading

Day 1: Psalm 119:160

Day 2: Ephesians 4:21–25

Day 3: John 8:32

Day 4: Deuteronomy 28:13

Day 5: 1 John 1:5–9

Day 6: Psalm 145

Day 7: Proverbs 14:1–7

Day 1: Psalm 119:160

Reflection

What does it mean that God's Word is true from the beginning?

Discussion

How can we apply the truth of God's Word in our daily lives?

Day 2: Ephesians 4:21–25

Reflection

What does it mean to "put off" the old self and "put on" the new self in Christ?

Discussion

How can we practically live out this transformation in our relationships and actions?

Day 3: John 8:32

Reflection

Contemplate the freedom that comes from knowing the truth.

Discussion

How can knowing and embracing the truth set us free in our lives? What is the connection between truth and freedom, as mentioned in this verse?

Day 4: Deuteronomy 28:13

Reflection

Consider the blessings of obedience mentioned in this verse.

Discussion

How does living according to God's ways lead to success and victory?

Day 5: 1 John 1:5-9

Reflection

What does it mean to walk in the light, confess our sins, and forgiveness in Christ?

Discussion

How does God's forgiveness and cleansing impact our relationship with Him?

Day 6: Psalm 145

Reflection

How can praising God for His attributes strengthen your faith?

Discussion

Share aspects of God's greatness and faithfulness that resonate with you.

Day 7: Proverbs 14:1–7

Reflection

Compare and contrast the wise and the foolish as described in these verses.

Discussion

What can we learn about the consequences of our words and actions?

NOTES

Chapter 3
Become Bulletproof

Wonder Woman used her bracelets to deflect bullets, but they were also meant to keep her strength to a manageable level and not to become enslaved to them. In a similar way, our emotions, if left unchecked, will lead us into a form of bondage to our feelings. We have a choice to either become enslaved to our emotions or protect the seat of our emotions—our hearts—by living a righteous life.

Being righteous doesn't mean we're more "holy" or better than anyone else; our good deeds are "as filthy rags" (Isa. 64:6, KJV). Our righteousness is given to us by a holy God; He alone is righteous. When we learn to wear His righteousness and give Jesus control over our hearts and emotions, then He can protect us from things that deeply wound our souls, including emotions such as condemnation, low self-esteem, depression, fear, anxiety, unforgiveness, and resentment. In a sense, we can become bulletproof.

Recommended Daily Reading

Day 1: Proverbs 4:23

Day 2: Romans 6:18; 15:13

Day 3: 2 Corinthians 10:4-5

Day 4: Ephesians 4:23-24

Day 5: Hebrews 4:12–13

Day 6: 1 Samuel 16:6–7

Day 7: Isaiah 61:3

Day 1: Proverbs 4:23

Reflection

Meditate on guarding your heart and its significance.

Discussion

Why is guarding your heart important in the Christian life? How can we actively guard our hearts from negative influences?

Day 2: Romans 6:18; 15:13

Reflection

Explore the connection between freedom, joy, and hope in Christ.

Discussion

How can a focus on God's hope fill us with joy and peace?

Day 3: 2 Corinthians 10:4-5

Reflection

Consider the thoughts you should've taken captive this week.

Discussion

How can we practically combat negative or harmful thoughts?

Day 4: Ephesians 4:23-24

Reflection

What does it mean to be renewed in the spirit of your mind?

Discussion

How can we actively put on the new self in Christ?

Day 5: Hebrews 4:12–13

Reflection

How does the Word of God serve as a discerning tool in our lives, thoughts, and intentions?

Discussion

In what ways can the Word of God help us understand our thoughts and intentions?

Day 6: 1 Samuel 16:6–7

Reflection

Consider God's perspective, looking at the heart rather than appearances.

Discussion

How can we avoid making judgments based solely on outward appearances?

Day 7: Isaiah 61:3

Reflection

Consider the symbolism of beauty for ashes and the oil of gladness. What does this phrase mean?

Discussion

How has God brought beauty and joy into your life through difficult circumstances?

NOTES

Chapter 4

Boots on the Ground

We are constantly under attack, and we have a weapon that places us on the defensive. We defend ourselves by assuming a "ready stance" to stand firmly on God's Word and understand His grace without abusing it. We should be ready to share His Word with others and tell them how it has worked in our lives.

Being a Christian doesn't give us the right to walk all over others or allow people to use us as doormats. We should, however, be ready at all times to take the "gospel of peace" to all mankind, whether in word or deed, and do it lightning fast. Don't second-guess—if you see an opportunity, take it!

Recommended Daily Reading

Day 1: John 14:26–27

Day 2: Isaiah 26:3

Day 3: John 16:33

Day 4: Philippians 4:6–7

Day 5: 1 Corinthians 14:33

Day 6: Isaiah 53:5

Day 7: Psalm 122

Day 1: John 14:26-27

Reflection

Jesus gives us His perfect peace through the person of the Holy Spirit. What is the significance of Jesus promising the Holy Spirit as our Helper and the peace He gives?

Discussion

How has the presence of the Holy Spirit brought peace into your life during challenging times?

Day 2: Isaiah 26:3

Reflection

Contemplate the perfect peace found in trusting in God. How does trust in God lead to perfect peace, according to this verse?

Discussion

Share examples of moments when your trust in God's sovereignty brought you peace in difficult situations.

Day 3: John 16:33

Reflection

In what ways does Jesus encourage us to take heart despite the troubles of the world?

Discussion

How can we find peace and courage in Christ when facing adversity?

Day 4: Philippians 4:6–7

Reflection

What does it mean to present our requests to God with thanksgiving for His peace to guard our hearts and minds?

Discussion

Share personal experiences of finding peace through prayer and thanksgiving.

Day 5: 1 Corinthians 14:33

Reflection

How does the God of order and peace relate to our interactions within the church and our personal lives?

Discussion

Discuss ways to promote peace and order in your church community and relationships.

Day 6: Isaiah 53:5

Reflection

Consider the significance of Christ's sacrifice for our healing and peace.

Discussion

How does the understanding of Jesus' sacrifice bring emotional and spiritual healing to our lives?

Day 7: Psalm 122

Reflection

Reflect on the joy of gathering in the house of the Lord, as described in this Psalm.

Discussion

Share the importance of corporate worship and fellowship in your spiritual journey.

Chapter 5

Take Up Your Shield

One of my favorite scenes in the 2017 *Wonder Woman* movie is when Diana ignores all the naysaying men, reveals her armor, climbs up a ladder, and rushes into battle in No Man's Land, using her shield to stand her ground, taking every hit to help the Allied soldiers.

A shield is an offensive and a defensive weapon in combat meant to protect against attacks and to safeguard a warrior as she charges into the heat of battle. Ephesians 6:16 says, "In addition to all this, take up the shield of faith, with which you can extinguish all the flaming arrows of the evil one." That phrase "in addition" means Paul was letting the believers in Ephesus know their faith was part of their weaponry, and that other pieces were needed to complement their faith.

Faith is absolutely essential if we're to stand firm against temptation, or "the fiery arrows of the devil." While the breastplate of righteousness protects our vital organs, especially our heart (the soul), the shield of faith is meant to deflect negative thoughts, negative words (whether spoken directly to us or behind our backs), and temptations that hit us straight on or that come out of left field.

As believers, faith is foundational to our walk with God. Why? Because "without faith, it is impossible to please God, because anyone who comes to him must believe that he exists and that he rewards those who earnestly seek him" (Heb. 11:6).

Recommended Daily Reading

Day 1: Isaiah 40:29

Day 2: Luke 5:17–20

Day 3: Psalm 57:7

Day 4: James 1:2–3

Day 5: James 4:7

Day 6: Hebrews 11

Day 7: Joshua 10

Day 1: Isaiah 40:29

Reflection

Are you currently going through a tough time? Journal your thoughts, meditate on this verse, declare the Word in prayer, and open your heart to God.

_____

_____

_____

_____

_____

_____

_____

_____

_____

Discussion

Share instances where you felt God's strength carry you through challenging times.

How does God's strength sustain us when we are weak?

Day 2: Luke 5:17–20

Reflection

What does the faith of the friends who brought the paralyzed man to Jesus teach us?

Discussion

How can our faith in Christ lead us to take bold actions to help others encounter Him?

Day 3: Psalm 57:7

Reflection

Think back to a time in your life when you were afraid and God miraculously intervened to restore your hope in Him.

Discussion

Share experiences of finding refuge in God during times of trouble or fear.

How does taking refuge in God relate to finding hope and security?

Day 4: James 1:2-3

Reflection

Think back to a time when you took notice of how God's joy overshadowed the trial you were experiencing at the time.

Discussion

How can we maintain joy and growth in faith amidst trials and testing?

What is the purpose of trials and the growth of faith, according to these verses?

Day 5: James 4:7

Reflection

Explore the connection between submitting to God and resisting the devil.

Discussion

Share practical ways to resist temptation and submit to God's will.

Day 6: Hebrews 11

Reflection
Study examples of faith in the lives of various biblical figures.

Discussion
Which biblical character's faith story resonates with you the most, and why?

Day 7: Joshua 10

Reflection

Reflect on God's faithfulness in fighting battles for His people.

Discussion

Share examples of times when God intervened in your life's challenges.

Chapter 6
Queen in Training

I had the opportunity to visit Greece—a beautiful country filled with lovely people, rich culture, and so much history. During the visit to ancient Olympia, I was able to tour a museum that houses relics, including ancient weapons and armor. During that visit, I learned that the bronze "Corinthian" helmet was the most widely used helmet in the archaic and early classical periods. Over time, the Greeks adjusted the anatomical details of the helmet to make it better fit the warrior's head.

Like the ancient Greek warriors, we have a helmet as part of our armor—it's called the helmet of salvation. It serves to protect our "head"—primarily our relationship with God and secondarily our households. If the head is wounded in battle, then the rest of the body can't function. Similarly, if our most critical relationship is damaged, everything in our lives, including every other relationship, will be affected. Speaking to all my "sisters in Christ," we are queens in training, and as such we should guard and carefully manage our salvation and relationship with God.

Recommended Daily Reading

Day 1: James 1:2-3, 12

Day 2: James 1:21–22

Day 3: Esther 2: 15-18

Day 4: Esther 4:11-14

Day 5: Ephesians 2:8

Day 6: Philippians 2:12-13

Day 7: Psalm 139:1–6, 13–17

Day 1: James 1:2-3, 12

Reflection

How does James view trials as an opportunity for joy and perseverance?

Discussion

Share a personal experience where facing a trial led to spiritual growth and endurance.

Day 2: James 1:21–22

Reflection

Explore the idea of receiving God's Word with meekness and being doers of the Word.

Discussion

How can we practically apply God's Word in our daily lives to live out our faith?

Day 3: Esther 2:15-18

Reflection

Consider Esther's preparation to meet the king and her character qualities.

Discussion

How can we develop qualities of character that honor God in our lives?

Day 4: Esther 4:11-14

Reflection

Reflect on Mordecai's challenge to Esther to rise up for such a time as this.

Discussion

Discuss the significance of recognizing God's providence and calling in our own lives.

Day 5: Ephesians 2:8

Reflection

What does it mean to be saved by grace through faith?

Discussion

Share how God's grace and faith have transformed your life.

Day 6: Philippians 2:12-13

Reflection

How do these verses emphasize the partnership between God's work and our obedience?

Discussion

How can we actively work out our salvation while relying on God's empowering grace?

Day 7: Psalm 139:1–6, 13–17

Reflection

Contemplate God's intimate knowledge of you as described in this Psalm.

Discussion

How does understanding God's deep knowledge of us impact our relationship with Him?

NOTES

Chapter 7

The "god" Killer

The sword described in Ephesians 6—the sword of the Spirit, which is the Word of God—is an offensive weapon against the enemy. We use it to kill the "gods" in our lives not by flashing it to the enemy but by releasing its truth into the atmosphere.

The Bible says God's Word will accomplish that for which it was sent (Isa. 55:10–11). When we declare God's Word, we not only remind ourselves of who we are in Him, but we deal devastating blows to our enemy. Instead of continuing to advance against us, he will have to retreat when we choose to believe and speak God's Word over ourselves and our situation.

Recommended Daily Reading

Day 1: Matthew 6:9–15

Day 2: Romans 8:24–28

Day 3: Daniel 6:8–28

Day 4: Daniel 10:7–15

Day 5: Luke 18:1–8

Day 6: Mark 11:24

Day 7: Luke 5:16

Day 1: Matthew 6:9-15

Reflection

Explore the Lord's Prayer and its significance in your relationship with God.

Discussion

Share how the Lord's Prayer has influenced your prayer life and relationship with God.

Day 2: Romans 8:24-28

Reflection

How does this passage offer hope and assurance in God's purposes?

Discussion

Share instances where you've seen God work all things for good in your life.

Day 3: Daniel 6:8-28

Reflection

Study the story of Daniel in the lion's den and his unwavering faith.

Discussion

How can we apply Daniel's commitment to prayer and faithfulness in our own lives?

Day 4: Daniel 10:7–15

Reflection

Explore Daniel's encounter with the angel and the spiritual battle.

Discussion

How does this passage reveal the spiritual realm's influence on our lives?

Day 5: Luke 18:1–8

Reflection

Discuss the parable of the persistent widow and the importance of persistent prayer.

Discussion

Share instances where persistent prayer led to answers and breakthroughs.

Day 6: Mark 11:24

Reflection

How does faith play a central role in prayer according to this verse?

Discussion

Discuss the relationship between faith and answered prayer in your life.

Day 7: Luke 5:16

Reflection

Examine Jesus' practice of withdrawing to pray and its importance.

Discussion

How can we prioritize regular times of solitude and prayer in our busy lives?

www.ingramcontent.com/pod-product-compliance
Lightning Source LLC
Chambersburg PA
CBHW080325080526
44585CB00021B/2474